CRIMSOC 5: 'Pathologising Youth Development and Risk'

Published in Los Angeles USA by CRIMSOC 2016

CRIMSOC 5: 'Pathologising Youth Development and Risk'

Authors:

Dr. Alina Haines, Health and Community Care Research Unit (HaCCRU), Institute of Psychology, Health and Society (IPHS), University of Liverpool, England, UK

Prof. Elizabeth Perkins, Health and Community Care Research Unit (HaCCRU), Institute of Psychology, Health and Society (IPHS), University of Liverpool, England, UK

Prof. Richard Whittington, (1) Brøset Centre for Research & Education in Forensic Psychiatry, St. Olav's Hospital & Department of Neuroscience, Norwegian University of Science & Technology (NTNU), Trondheim, Norway; (2) HaCCRU, Institute of Psychology, Health and Society (IPHS), University of Liverpool, UK

Corresponding author

Dr. Alina Haines, Health and Community Care Research Unit (HaCCRU), Eleanor Rathbone Building, University of Liverpool, Liverpool L69 7ZQ, United Kingdom, Email: a.haines@liv.ac.uk, Tel 0044 (0)151 794 2945

Funding

Department of Health (no grant number)

Acknowledgements

This article is informed by a broader two-year evaluative research project that was funded by the Department of Health and conducted by a multi-disciplinary research team from the University of Liverpool comprising: Barry Goldson, Alina Haines, Alan Haycox, Rachel Houten, Steven Lane, Rajan Nathan, James McGuire, Elizabeth Perkins, and Richard Whittington (PI). The authors wish to thank colleagues in the research team for their valuable contribution to this research project and the youth justice liaison and diversion (YJLD) teams for their support with the research and data collection.

About the Authors:

Alina Haines is a post doctoral researcher at the Health and Community Care Research Unit (HaCCRU), the University of Liverpool, England, UK. In the last 10 years, Alina has conducted social research focusing on youth justice, offender rehabilitation and violence prevention. She is currently working in collaboration with Mersey Care NHS Trust, initiating and managing research projects in the area of mental health and forensic mental health.

Elizabeth Perkins holds the William VI Chair of Community Nursing research and is the Director of the Health and Community Care Research Unit at the University of Liverpool, England, UK. She has been undertaking social research for over thirty years with a particular expertise in the use of qualitative methodologies. She has undertaken a number of studies in the field of mental health including an evaluation of decision making in mental health review tribunals and an exploration of the use of restraint. She is currently undertaking an evaluation of the way in which the Care Quality Commission is implementing its new inspection procedures.

Richard Whittington is Professor of Mental Health at the Norwegian University of Science and Technology (NTNU), Trondheim, Norway, and the University of Liverpool, England, UK. He is also a researcher at the Brøset Centre for Research & Education in Forensic Psychiatry, St. Olavs University Hospital in Trondheim and an Honorary Research Fellow with Mersey Care NHS Trust. He has a longstanding interest in the prevention and management of antisocial, aggressive and otherwise risky behaviour associated with mental health problems amongst adults and young people and has published extensively on these topics.

The Health & Community Care Unit (HaCCRU) was established in 1993 and includes a group of social scientists engaged in high quality health services research and dissemination. Researchers in HaCCRU have backgrounds in sociology, social policy, psychology and criminology, applying theories and methods from these disciplines to understand health care processes and to improve health service delivery. The centre has been commissioned by a range of agencies in government and the private and voluntary sectors to design, implement and disseminate independent research relevant to real-life problems and service delivery challenges. Link to HaCCRU: https://www.liverpool.ac.uk/psychology-health-and-society/research/health-and-community-care/about/

Abstract:

Pathologising growing up:

The re-construction of risky behaviour as mental illness?

Background.

Many aspects of daily life have become medicalised these days. The latest revision of the predominant psychiatric classification system, DSM-V, has generated significant controversy amongst professionals, sociological thinkers, and service users because of the way in which new specific diagnoses have been added. One of the major debates has been around diagnosing Attention Deficit Hyperactivity Disorder (ADHD). However, irrespective of whether the disruptive behaviour associated with a diagnosis of ADHD is a manifestation of mental disorder or not, it is a common feature amongst youth and adult offender populations. Recognition of this association between a set of behaviours and certain outcomes, together with application of the medicalization concept, has led to the development worldwide of youth justice diversion programmes which aim to identify young people who have come to the attention of the police but whose problems are considered to be mental health vulnerabilities rather than moral deficiencies requiring punishment and/or rehabilitation.

Methods.

In this paper we draw on data gathered from an evaluation of a Youth Justice Liaison Diversion (YJLD) pilot scheme in England, UK, to explore the way in which the 'risky' behaviours of some young people can become defined as mental health issues. The data reported here were gathered from 24 interviews with children and young people aged between 11 and 17 years old and engaging with the YJLD scheme, and 25 interviews with professional stakeholders collaborating with the scheme.

Results.

Findings suggest that, while the anti-social behaviour of the young people interviewed was perceived as problematic to society and to some parents, it was viewed as a relatively normal part of growing up by the young people themselves, and their peer group. Mental health professionals talked about the stigma of mental health and the difficulty in engaging families with services, but also recognised that the complexity of social and familial problems underpinning young people's lives could explain their vulnerabilities and emotional issues, contributing to or resulting in their offending behaviour.

Perspectives and future research.

This paper argues that the value of orienting young people toward the mental health system rather than the criminal justice system depends on the perspective adopted. Treating people and their behaviours with medication and therapy versus incarcerating them represents two ends of a spectrum. Tackling the fundamental inequalities which exist in society and which remain inextricably linked to the kind of future that young people can access may help prevent the emergence of some of these behaviours but rely on investment of huge resources and political will. As this study was limited by the small number of interviews and a convenience sample, future qualitative research should try to build on it and unearth the ways in which 'mental health' or 'offending' labels affect young people's own perceptions and lives.

Key words: Adolescence, intervention, mental health, social construction of mental illness

Introduction

The process of medicalization is one in which individual behaviours and lifestyles become interpreted as manifestations of illness requiring medical intervention of some sort. It is a process that has been subjected to examination since at least the development of the anti-psychiatry critique of the 1960's. Examples and explanations of medicalization have multiplied since that time indicating that the process is far more complex than set out in the original critique. This critique tended to portray medicalization as a binary, all-or-nothing event imposed on vulnerable groups by more powerful interests with inevitably negative long-term consequences for the recipients. There was furthermore an assumption that medicine and quasi-medicine such as psychiatry were always expanding their scope to include wider types of behaviour.

Social constructionism provides a counterpoint to medicine's largely deterministic approaches to disease and illness, emphasising how the meaning and experience of illness is shaped by social interactions, shared cultural traditions, shifting frameworks of knowledge, and relations of power. The social constructionist approach to illness differentiates between disease (the biological condition) and illness (the social meaning of the condition) (Eisenberg, 1977). 'Illness is a social designation', as Gusfield argues (1967: 180), and while biophysiological bodily conditions or naturally occurring events occur, these are not *ipso facto* illnesses, nor diseases. Early sociological thinkers and adepts of social constructionism argued that illness and disease, like deviance, are social constructions, and recognised the real social consequences of an illness label (Becker, 1963; Spector and Kitsuse, 1977; Freidson, 1970; Foucault, 1977). From a constructionist standpoint, illnesses have both biomedical and experiential dimensions; the cultural and social meanings attributed to certain illnesses have an impact on the way the illness is experienced, depicted, and the social response to it (Schneider and Conrad, 1983).

Medicalization – as the social construction of medical knowledge – has been studied and criticised by sociologists over the years, with early studies focusing on medicalization of deviance, including 'madness', drug and alcohol problems, and homosexual behaviour (Conrad and Schneider, 1992). During the following decades, sociologists have focused on the medicalization of natural phenomenon (such as pregnancy, childbirth, menstruation) (Barker 1998; Riessman 1983; Riska 2003) and ordinary life events (Conrad, 2007). But medicalization is expanding further, beyond medical professionals and social movements, to consumers and the industry, especially the pharmaceutical industry. There is a recognition that a range of stakeholders beyond the medical profession have an interest in both applying and resisting the application of medical categories and the classification might involve a process of negotiation between interested parties. Potential stakeholders include the 'patient' him/herself and those who provide informal care for them, i.e. parents, the wider family, and the society. The acceptance and incorporation of a medicalised identity by the individual, when classified by a professional, is thus an active process of personal acceptance or resistance.

The latest revision of one of the two predominant psychiatric classification systems, DSM-V (APA 2013), is the leading contemporary statement of medicalization and lists over 200 distinct categories grouped into 22 broad groups. It sets out which individual behaviours and social phenomena are currently claimed (and not claimed) by the psychiatric profession as mental disorders. Whilst it is a purely American product, it has global influence. It is designed as a guide to psychiatric diagnostic (Frances and Widiger, 2012) and does not explicitly address any questions of aetiology. However, inclusion within the manual defines or 'labels' a behaviour or lifestyle as a form of mental disorder which implies that the medical profession have primary jurisdiction over managing it.

Ben Zeev et al. (2010) argue that understanding labels is fundamental to understanding the stigma of mental illness. Publication of DSM-V has generated significant controversy amongst professionals and service users (British Psychological Society, 2011; Giles, 2013) because of the way in which new specific diagnoses have been added. As Dowrick and Frances explore in their article on depression (2013) the impact of adopting a broad definition of depression is that many more people get diagnosed and treated with antidepressants, so much so that rates of prescribing of antidepressant medication doubled in the UK between 1998 and 2010. In the US 11% of the population aged over 11 now takes an antidepressant. Evidence from clinical trials, however, suggests that, in the case of mild depression at least, antidepressants have little or no effect (Turner et al., 2008; Gibbons et al., 2012).

One of the major debates has been around diagnosing Attention Deficit Hyperactivity Disorder (ADHD) and this is a good exemplar of modern medicalization. The diagnostic criteria for ADHD in DSM-V are essentially the same as in the previous version, but some proposals, such as the addition of new impulsivity symptoms and a reduction in the number of required symptoms (to qualify for certain diagnoses) were contentious (Coghill and Seth, 2011). ADHD is already the most prevalent diagnosis amongst children with 8% of those aged 8-15 years meeting the diagnostic criteria over 12 months in a community survey (Merikangas et al., 2010). Other disorder, i.e. mood, conduct, anxiety and eating disorders are all much less common amongst children (<3%). The amendments to the diagnostic criteria for ADHD exemplify the expansion of medicalization since the 1950s, with an original focus exclusively on overactive schoolboys extending now to being an attention disorder which can emerge and persist anywhere in the lifespan from the age of 2 to adulthood (Conrad and Slodden, 2013). This expansion in the diagnostic focus reflects, amongst other things, marketing pressures from pharmaceutical companies and lobbying by adult ADHD 'consumer' groups and parents of disruptive children for access to medication.

Regardless of whether the disruptive behaviour associated with a diagnosis of ADHD is a manifestation of mental disorder or not, it is a common feature amongst youth and adult offender populations and it is up to nine times more common in young offenders than amongst young non-offenders (Satterfield et al., 1994; Harpin and Young, 2012). Recognition of this association between a set of behaviours and certain outcomes, together with application of the medicalization concept, has led to the development worldwide of youth justice diversion programmes which aim to identify young people who have come to the attention of the police but whose problems are considered to be mental health vulnerabilities rather than moral deficiencies requiring punishment and/or rehabilitation. The political aspiration to classify in this way may be pragmatically focused on improving social and economic outcomes or driven by concern for the individual (or both). However, regardless of the motivation, the classification itself will have consequences for the recipient and their families and thus may be welcomed, resisted or ignored by them.

An opportunity arose to examine the responses of young people and their families to their referral to a new youth diversion scheme in England which aimed to identify a wide range of vulnerabilities, with an emphasis on mental health issues amongst children and people in contact with the criminal justice system. This paper reports on the impact of this government initiative to identify mental health needs and vulnerabilities in young people engaged in risky and potentially criminal activities, and explores the balance of resistance and acceptance amongst the recipients.

Youth Justice Liaison and Diversion in England

Numerous reports have highlighted a wide range of unmet complex needs of children and young people at various points in the youth justice system (e.g. Lader et al., 2000; Harrington and Bailey, 2005; Goldson, 2002, 2006; HMCIP, 2006; Solomon and Garside, 2008; Lancet, 2009 and HM Government, 2009). It is argued that rates of mental health problems, learning difficulties and other vulnerabilities among these young people are roughly double those of children in the general population (e.g. Mental Health Foundation, 2002; Hagell, 2002; Chitsabesan et al., 2006; Healthcare Commission, 2006 and 2009). The Ministry of Justice Green Paper, 'Breaking the Cycle: Effective punishment, rehabilitation and sentencing of Offenders (2010) and the government strategy 'No health without mental health' (HM Government, 2011) highlight that '...early interventions, particularly with vulnerable children and young people, can improve lifetime health and wellbeing, prevent mental illness and reduce costs incurred by ill health, unemployment and crime (HM Government, 2011: 9).

This growing body of evidence led to the testing out of a model to improve early identification and support of mental health needs and other vulnerabilities in the Youth Justice System (YJS). The concept of diversion used by policy makers and politicians included:

- Diversion away from the YJS towards mental health, emotional support and welfare systems (taking into account proportionality, public interest and risk management issues);

- Enhanced post-arrest and pre-court activity to meet the full range of needs of vulnerable young people in a more appropriate and timely manner;

- Diversion within the YJS, where appropriate, away from custodial settings;

- More efficient transfer processes from custodial settings into secure psychiatric settings where necessary.

The Department of Health for England funded six pilot sites to help test out and develop a Youth Justice Liaison and Diversion (YJLD) scheme to enhance health provision in their Youth Offending Services (YOS). The scheme was initially funded between December 2008 and March 2012 and an evaluation was commissioned by the Department of Health during the same time. The evaluation included examination of changes in reoffending and mental health outcomes after contact with the scheme, a health economic analysis examining its relative costs and benefits, and a qualitative study of the perspectives of service users and providers on the value (and limitations) of the scheme (Haines et al., 2012). This paper focuses on the way young people talked about their circumstances and their experience of the criminal justice system, but also includes the views of diversion workers and key stakeholders collaborating with the scheme. The paper also explores the implications of labelling the behaviours which resulted in their contacts with the youth justice system as mental health issues.

Methods

The qualitative data reported here are based on data from interviews with children and stakeholders. Twenty-four interviews were conducted with children and young people aged between 11 and 17 years old who were in contact with the YJLD scheme. Sixteen (67%) were male and eight were female. All children and their parents/guardians gave informed written consent prior to the interview. The interviews took place in the young people's home or at the relevant diversion offices, or at the young person's school. Where necessary, the child or the young person was accompanied by a carer or a parent. The interviews explored the young people's perspectives and experiences with reference to the following areas:

- Their sense of belonging, social circumstances and contact with the criminal justice system as well as any other social issues;

- Their perspectives and experiences of formal education systems and, where appropriate, employment opportunities;

- Their conceptualisations of the future and their hopes, aspirations and ambitions.

Twenty-five interviews were conducted with twenty-nine professional stakeholders, including police officers; Youth Offending Team officers (social workers, education and health professionals), Child and Adolescent Mental Health Services (CAMHS) staff; representatives from the Crown Prosecution Service; psychologists, psychiatrists, psychotherapists; and, a representative from the Ministry of Justice. The interviews explored in main stakeholders' views and experience regarding the value and practice of youth diversion. All interviews were conducted by a university researcher following the appropriate ethical approvals and procedures.

The qualitative data derived from the interviews were analysed using Charmaz's principles of grounded theory (Charmaz, 2006). This approach is based on the idea that 'knowledge' is constructed and embedded in human perception and social experience. Studies informed by the principles of grounded theory tend to be focused on understanding social processes or actions. The topic guides used in this study for the interviews allowed respondents the scope to explore in detail their everyday experiences of being a young person growing up in their environment. The data were coded using the ideas of open coding and constant comparative analysis. Similarities and differences across the data were explored as the data were coded and compared, sometimes word by word or line by line. Concepts and categories were produced and patterns established which helped to explain the development of a range of core categories within the different data sets.

In addition, we draw on some of the quantitative data reported in the evaluation report, to provide a context for the qualitative findings. The data were collected via the project's information system used by all sites and developed as a means of collecting information on YJLD throughput and activity within the six sites. These contextual quantitative results will be provided first. The detailed results of the other components of the evaluation (e.g. mental health and reoffending outcomes) have been reported elsewhere (Haines et al., 2015; Whittington, Haines, and McGuire, 2015).

Contextual findings

All six pilot sites adopted slightly different approaches to diversion. The YJLD teams were based within the local authority Youth Offending Service (YOS) and/or the Child and Adolescent Mental Health Service (CAMHS). In essence, however, all schemes operated in and around police custody with YJLD workers being informed of young people who had been arrested. The teams offered their service to children and young people who were given a reprimand or a final warning, and low level offending, although one of the pilot sites covered more serious offences as well. A total of 1027 young people were referred to YJLD between December 2008 and August 2011 (33 months). The young people referred to the scheme were predominantly male (71%), White British or Northern European (67%), with an average age of 14.7 (10-17) years.

A third of young people referred directly engaged with the scheme, while 27% were screened for specific vulnerabilities and a full mental health assessment was conducted for 13%. These vulnerabilities were identified using a variety of screening and assessment tools, each site using YOT and/or CAMHS specific tools or locally adapted tools. Examples include: the Screening Questionnaire Interview for

Adolescents (SQifA); the Health the Nation Outcome Scales for Adolescents (HoNOSCA); an extended/CAMHS version of SQIfA, the Screening Interview for Adolescents (SifA); the NHS CAMHS Common Assessment Framework (CAF); the CAMHS assessment; the Strengths and Difficulties Questionnaires (SDQ); the Structured Assessment of Violence Risk in Youth (SAVRY); the Juvenile Sex Offender Assessment Protocol II (J-SOAP II); the Psychopathy Checklist, Revised assessment (PCL-R) and the Learning Disability Screening Questionnaire (LDSQ).

As indicated in Table 1 below, the majority of the concerns identified by the YJLD workers in the young people were behavioural and social issues. Only a minority of young people 15.4% had an identifiable and diagnosable mental health issue. These young people were identified with 1.2 mental health issues per person on average and the largest proportion of these were linked to ADHD (39%), followed by conduct disorder and autism (both at 19%).

Wider area of concern	Specific vulnerabilities	Frequency (n)	Percent (%)
Mental health issues 28.4%	**Suspected diagnosable mental health problem**	**158**	**15.40**
	Parent with mental health problems	57	5.60
	Non severe pathology (e.g. anxiety, worry)	76	7.40
Behavioural issues 69.0%	Anger/aggression	380	37.00
	Behavioural problems	329	32.00
Social issues 51.6%	Family conflict	258	25.00
	Association with gang/violent peer group	132	13.00
	Poor relationships/lack of friends	97	9.40
	Victim of bullying/harassment	43	4.20
Safeguarding issues 36.8%	Neglect/insufficient parenting	75	7.30
	Domestic violence	70	6.80
	Risk of self harm/suicide	57	5.60
	Foster Care/Childrens' home	44	4.30
	Safeguarding needs	42	4.10
	Homelessness/accommodation difficulties	37	3.60
	Sexual abuse/exploitation	36	3.50
	Physical abuse	16	1.60
Developmental issues 19.2%	Suspected Learning/intellectual disability	48	4.70
	Possible speech and communication needs	20	1.90
	Poor school attendance	129	12.60
Wellbeing/confidence issues	Unhappy, dissatisfied, low self esteem	124	12.10
Substance misuse issues	Substance misuse	120	11.70
None	None	117	11.40
Other issues	Other	18	1.80
Physical health issues	Physical health needs	10	1.00
TOTAL		2493	n/a

Qualitative findings:

Young people's perspective

From the twenty four young people who were interviewed, the overwhelming majority (n=19) lived in households headed by a single parent (n=16 with lone-parent mothers and n=3 with lone-parent fathers). Almost all of the young people interviewed reported some form of household disharmony - including that resulting from their contact with the youth justice system or problems at school. Offences reported by the young people ranged from shoplifting and stealing to assault. This was a diverse group with a myriad of difficult circumstances and vulnerabilities relating variously to: socio-economic hardship; problematic familial and/or social relations; disrupted education pathways; social welfare needs; safeguarding issues; alcohol misuse; behavioural problems; anger management issues; unresolved questions deriving from bereavement, grief and loss and bullying and victimisation.

All of the young people interviewed lived in areas of multiple socio-economic deprivation. Many described their neighbourhoods and communities as 'bad areas'. Some young people talked about strategies for limiting their physical presence in that geographical space.

When I go out I try to get away from the area; I try to go away from here. (Female, age 16)

Round here's not very nice is it? [I] haven't really got any friends round here… I don't like it round here… so I just pull away and become a recluse… I don't really go out around here because most of them do drugs and all that and get into trouble and I don't want to do that anymore, so I just like keep myself to myself and stuff like that. (Male, age 15)

While other young people linked place with friendship and behaviour. These young people described being more embedded in their neighbourhood through attachment to their friends who also lived locally. However, many of these young people reported a separation between their lives with their friends and their lives within the family. Parents were reported to have issues with their friends who were often seen to be a bad influence.

My dad thinks they are bad people and everything 'cause they haven't got an education and so on and so forth and I am like 'yeah but they are my friends, I talk to them, I can talk to them about anything'. I talk to them but then yeah my mum and dad think just 'cause they are older than me they are going to take me into bad things like kind of thing. (Male, age 15)

I have good friends. I've got a lot of good friends but my parents don't see it like that because of who my good friends are... how can I put it, they're classed as dangerous people and I've got a lot of friends like that and yes maybe they're not nice people, but they've always been good to me. (Male, age 17)

Ties to friends eclipsed their social circumstances highlighting the difficulties that arise in changing behaviour while a young person remains living 'at home'. A few young people who were trying to reform their behaviour reported feeling quite isolated and peculiarly out-of-place within their immediate geographic locales through attempting to 'break free' from their previous lives..

The majority of the young people in the sample had had previous contact with the police. Among their friendship circles it was neither uncommon nor problematic to have spent a night in the police cells. It was a normative experience for young people, the thing they often held in common with their friends. Friendships in this group of young people were conceptualised as both risky and supportive.

INT What do your friends think about finding out you've been in trouble with the police?

They don't mind. Most of them have been in trouble. Most of them have like been in police cells way more than me. Like some of my mates have actually just started going into prison already. So it's like ... it's not like something that you do to look popular, but if you have you've got something to talk about with them... like when I first met like my mate... yes my boyfriend, Daniel, that was just like the conversation. It was like 'Have you ever been arrested?' 'Yes'. 'Have you?' 'Yes' and we like got along and just started talking like how many times did you count. Then just like saying stuff like that. It was just like a conversation to start, otherwise if it wasn't then we'd just be sitting there like yeah… it's like most of the people that I like it's like a daily thing, it's not a big thing, so it's like a conversation like going to the shop. Like 'What shop did you go to?' 'What police station did you go?' So it's more like that. (Female, age 15)

The young people interviewed in this study were a highly heterogeneous group with regard to their reported mental health status. Whilst there was evidence of myriad difficult circumstances and vulnerabilities, only very few of the young people interviewed had a mental (ill) health diagnosis. Many young people had been referred to children and adolescent mental health services for assessment and/or treatment, and several of the conversations during interview alluded to learning difficulties, anxiety, depression, ADHD, OCD, autism, hearing voices and other 'disorders'. There was, however, little detailed understanding of their mental health diagnoses and of its relationship to their behaviour.

I don't think it's made much change but I've seen another doctor here... they told me I've got ADD and ADHD and OCD.

INT Do you like all these letters?

Yes. I've got it [all], right. Before I came here I was told I had provisional defiant disorder and conduct disorder. But I've got ADHD and OCD... and I hate my tablets.

INT What tablets do you know?

I can't remember what they are but... everyone thinks they're totally rubbish and they can make me ill. (Male, age 11)

Young people referred to YJLD often received some mental health input and this was often for anger management. A significant number of the children and young people interviewed articulated difficulties in controlling anger, often with violent consequences. Interestingly, there was little evidence of bravado in such accounts; violence was seemingly perceived either with a sense of resigned acceptance or as a product of uncontrollable impulse, as illustrated in the following quote.

I just get angry. Like when I get angry I like usually take it out on things around me. Like I try my best not to hit people but sometimes I get to the point where I do... I used to have like loads of fights at school but nowadays I just... try and control my anger but... sometimes I don't control it and I take it out on people I don't even know... like random people in the street... I get angry and then I start punching walls and shouting... It hurts if I punch something but like I broke my hand... I broke that getting angry. I got angry and punched a floor and broke it, it snapped... [Once] I was having a bad day at school and I got into trouble... I was really annoyed and moody and then I went into town... I don't know like I just switched, I went from being in a bad mood to really really angry and beat him up but then the Police were standing right behind me and I tried to run away but they were on bikes so they caught up with me. (Male, age 15)

Two young people highlighted the role of alcohol in their behaviour and anger management.

It's because I used to drink and then go out fighting, looking for fights and stuff. I still drink but I just don't go looking for fights and all that. I'd rather just stay in... I used to drink near enough every day... I don't do drugs though. (Male, age 16)

Well I have been trying to stop drink 'cause that gets me angry 'cause I went to a friend's party a month or two or so ago and then erm... erm... I was drinking and then I got angry and I punched a hole in her wall and she wasn't too happy so I have tried to stop drinking. (Male, age 15)

In another case a young boy talked about the difficulties he was experiencing coming to terms with his father's illness and reported that jokes or humorous comments about his father often provoked an angry and violent response.

INT Why do you say that your dad is a problem?

Cause he is quite ill... he's had like a lot of operations and stuff to try and fix his heart and stuff and they have not been like minor operations they have been like life threatening operations so... it's just like the worry of ... waking up and him not being there like... and ... I think that's how I get into trouble most really, like people trying to say something about my dad, like as a joke, but I don't find it a joke at all if anyone says anything about my dad. ... there was probably erm about a 95% chance that I would flip at someone if they said anything about my dad... But like around the time I had just got arrested my dad had just come out of hospital and ... I had just got kicked out of school and my dad just come out of hospital and my nan had a stroke and... everything was going on at the time... (Male, age 15)

While it was apparent in the interviews that the family and social circumstances of the young people contributed to their behaviour, it was unclear how reframing the behaviour as a mental health issue could be helpful. However, there were circumstances in which parents welcomed a medical diagnosis and its attendant treatment believing that it offered a relatively straightforward solution to complex behavioural problems. In the following quote, despite the young boy's dislike of the medication, there was a belief that the tablets made the child calmer.

INT   Did he [the YJLD worker] help you in any way?

Mother   I don't think it's made much change but then he's seen another doctor here which ... they finally assessed him and he's got [unclear] and ADHD.

YP   They [my tablets] make me sick.

Mother   No they don't really, they make you feel a bit sick but you ain't had no really bad side effects.

YP   No but ...

Mother   Actually quite a few adults have said to me, 'Oh no you don't want him on that one, get him on a different one, that's really bad', but he's ain't had no bad side effects. If they were that bad they wouldn't have put him on them […] [You're] a lot calmer.

YP   You think I'm calm?

Mother   I think you're a lot calmer yes. (Male, age 12, and his mother)

For the young people, however, their diversion into mental health services was perplexing. They seemed uncertain about the link between their 'criminal behaviour' and for example the 'talking therapies' that they received. They were quick to point out that, however enjoyable, their contact with the YJLD services was short lived, and in any case they always had to return to their communities and 'bad areas'.

I'm on my final warning... But I can't remember why.... I just sit down and talk about what my behaviour had been like and how my anger has been doing. I don't know whether that's called therapy or not.... (Male, age 15)

...they're all just like 'Well we'll take you out for an hour and bring you back' and it's just taking you out and getting you away and then bringing you back to the same problems, it's not like it's helping you. It's just distracting you for a couple of hours. So I don't see what the point is really. (Male, age 15)

Caught between their long standing family and social circumstances and the lives they had carved out for themselves, there was little room for imagining how their lives could be transformed. Strong hopes were articulated for an easier life, but this was not seen as something they alone could deliver. As the following quote highlights, there was an emphasis on the need for help, but also a desire to be recognised and understood as an adult.

I don't know to tell you the truth, I wouldn't really know what to do to try and help myself out... I don't have a clue what would make me stop. I think it's just the fact that I've been in trouble that many times now I've started to realise that it's not worth it anymore. I just want an easy life. I don't know. I just hope these things work... Because at the end of the day it's their job to know what they're on about, it's their job to help people, so they know what they're doing... if they know what they're doing hopefully they'll be able to help me and maybe help me to come to a point where I'm not going to get myself in as much trouble any more. It's mainly I want people to understand me, see where I'm coming from, see my point of view. Not just to turn round and go 'No you're wrong, you're in the wrong, you're in the wrong' all the time. I want people to understand me, treat me like I'm an adult not a little kid. (Male, aged 17).

Professional stakeholders' perspective

Professionals in this study suggested that mental health problems were less of an issue than the complexity of social and familial problems that these young people faced as part of their everyday lives. A representative from the Crown Prosecution Service (CSP) argued that there was too much emphasis on mental health:

R1   I think sometimes perhaps there is a ... perhaps tendency is the wrong word, but people are looking for mental health issues and I mean the sad reality is that the vast majority of youths that come through the Youth Court have issues that they wouldn't be there otherwise. I mean I can count on the space of one hand in 8 years the time the suspects come in with two parents in a happy, supportive house, where there are no drink or drug issues, no domestic violence issues or anything else, the vast majority of these people have issues and I wonder sometimes whether there's a ... [...] over-emphasis. (CPS representative)

Similarly, the YJLD workers from one of the pilot sites suggested that the social problems facing the young people were central to understanding their behaviour. They also argued that the behavioural and emotional issues were probably just a 'normal' response to life and growing up events such as school and problems with friends,, bereavement, or to more complex problems within the family

– mental health problems, abuse, violence – and a lack of adequate parenting:

R2   It's a lot of societal issues, emotional issues, there is very few, I don't know what she has told you, but there is very few mental health. (YJLD worker, YOT)

R3   ... I think it's, 'cause with young people you don't really see the sort of things like psychosis and serious depression in a lot of young people. It's very few numbers really. You are looking at sort of more behavioural developed mental disorders, mild anxiety, mild depression, those sorts of things that a transition times. You know like children might lose somebody or they might transfer to High School or they have friendship issues or they live in a chaotic family. Well in and out of that life depending on how the family circumstances. I am thinking of a boy that we went to see that lives up the road, his mum has mental health problems. Well he's not got mental health problems, he's got emotional problems because of his lifestyle, he's lived with a mum that's been very unwell with mental health wise. He's got siblings there; he's got abusive partners that have come in and out, still coming in and out smashing up the place and beating up mum. He's got no stability there has he?

INT No.

R3 Well children need stability so if you shake that stability then you are going to get some emotional problems and behavioural problems cause they don't know how to cope with it. So I would say they are more normal sort of reactions to a very difficult situation rather than say they are a mental health problem. (YJLD worker, CAMHS)

Professionals – especially the YJLD workers - talked about the stigma attached to mental health services and the difficulties they face when trying to engage families, especially children and young people, on the basis of a mental health diagnosis.

R6   [...] because a lot of the times we are kind of represented in a way, quite wrongfully by our title. Which is Mental Health Worker. And as soon as a child hears that term Mental Health Worker, automatically they have got this negative view of what we might be doing or what might, how we might be representing them. (YJLD worker, CAMHS)

R8   ... one of the first things is that we're a mental health service and a defence that that kind of brings up ... not just for parents but for young people as well [...] ... it kind of overshadows a lot of stuff and I don't know, we can't get away from that. We can't get away from that. (YJLD worker, CAMHS)

R9   ... I think the clinical aspect of the service can be quite scary to young people and all the stigmas that exist for adults around mental health exist tenfold to the young people. (YJLD worker, CAMHS)

Professionals reported that families were sensitive about receiving Mental Health Services visits to their homes for many reasons, including bad experiences in the past, or the stigma of mental health contact. But they did recognise that it was difficult to justify a mental health focused intervention in cases of minor offending which might be easier to attribute to growing up rather than mental health issues.

R11 [...] I don't see a huge amount of benefit in sending out an offer of a mental health screening to someone who's got a reprimand for pinching a chocolate bar from Tesco. I know in the past when we've offered appointments to ... I think it was a young girl who had had a fight at school and she'd got a reprimand and an angry parent phoned up and said 'Do you really think this is necessary to come and do a mental health screening just because my daughter had a fight at school'. You know, kids fight. So although you know there's still lots of people being arrested all the time, some of the offences you can't really justify and offer a service to.

[...] Yes I think the difficulty for us, because we are CAMHS workers, we're mental health nurses so we look at it from a mental health perspective, although we are looking for other vulnerabilities and it's a very comprehensive assessment that we would do with someone. The letter headed paper alone we sent out says Child and Adolescent Mental Health on it and, to a parent who's got a 12 years old who's stolen a chocolate bar it must be horrifying to think 'Goodness me, is this what it's come to?'

[...] I mean one parent did actually say 'You say my daughter's mental because that's what it says on this letter headed papers –mental health services'. (YJLD worker, CAMHS)

Consultant psychiatrists and psychologists interviewed in relation to the youth diversion scheme share similar views about the stigma of mental health.

R12 The kids that we try to work with, fundamentally, don't want to see us. They don't. Either because of the stigma as I said earlier, or a lack of insight, or a perception about what it is to be in touch with these do good-ers. (Psychiatrist, CAMHS)

They also stressed how the mental health label could be perceived as racist.

R13 And actually, just thinking of way back into the kind of ... you know way back into the mists of time, it wasn't easy for CAMHS and ASK to talk and there wasn't enough referrals and the YOS had a belief that particularly with black young men it would be racist to kind of put a mental health label on them. (Psychologist, CAMHS)

[...] And that's certainly something that we understand as a service. You know there's a lot of thinking around kind of race and mental health within the service, but there were those beliefs that got in the way of referrals way back and I think that there's been a lot of work from [name] and from the team, and from the YOS of making that communication better.

R12 [...]... we are in a borough where you are dealing with extremely disenfranchised youths, a lot of them are very gang affiliated, they are mostly young black men and they mostly have inherited an extremely adverse view of what it is to be seen by a psychiatrist at the worst level, but also anything to do with mental health. And we have to live that every day in our work with young people. (Psychiatrist, CAMHS)

Discussion

According to Szasz (1960), the term 'mental illness' is a misnomer. Mental illness is not illness per se. It is rather a form of cultural deviation – a failure, whether voluntary or not, to conform to normal physical and psychological behavioural expectations. In this context, the concept is used to refer to 'problems of living' so severe, wayward, or disturbing, for the individual or society, that they are not treated as falling within the more ordinary, acceptable miseries and difficulties of human life. It can be seen in this study that while the behaviours of these young people were perceived as problematic to society and to some parents, they were viewed as a relatively normal part of growing up by their peer group.

While this in itself may be a reflection of their lives, it also raises questions about any labelling of these behaviours or experiences as mental health issues. In this context the labelling may in the short term provide a passport to treatment and help but in the longer term a stigma which at some later date has negative consequences for the individual.

There is overwhelming evidence that many mental health issues are underpinned by a whole range of complex social and psychological factors. Turning life stresses or 'risky' adolescent behaviour into mental health problems could be perceived as an example of medical intrusion onto personal emotions (Horwitz and Wakefield, 2007). And, as we have seen from the quotes included in this paper, some families do not understand nor welcome this type of intervention.

The mental health professionals interviewed in this study also recognised that the complexity of social and familial problems underpinning young people's lives could explain their vulnerabilities and emotional issues, contributing to or resulting in their offending behaviour. The YJLD scheme was developed within the context of a broader psychosocial understanding of antisocial and criminal behaviour in which punishment was not viewed as an appropriate, effective or a desirable response. The scheme forms part of a wider policy to bring mental health services and the criminal justice system closer together and in some cases to converge (Rutherford, 2010). Although the scheme did not in any way explicitly aim to increase formal diagnoses of mental health disorders, by highlighting 'problematic' adolescent behaviour as a potential mental health issue, it created a situation in which individuals were not encouraged to see themselves as the architects of their lives, further detracting from any sense of agency they may have been able to develop (Dowrick, 2009). The young people in this study did not perceive the stigma of offending to be nearly as great as that arising from a mental health diagnosis. In attempting to understand offending behaviour as a mental health issue there is a danger that young people acquire the stigma of a mental illness label and are encouraged to look to psychiatry and pharmacology to solve their problems.

Sociologists argue that one of the undesirable outcomes of medicalization is that it encourages medical solutions while overlooking the social context of complicated problems (Lantz, Uchtenstein, and Pollack, 2007). When difficulties in children's attention and behaviour get defined as ADHD, current policies encourage the use of medication and special accommodation in schools for learning disabled students; but these responses fail to address the social and non-medical reasons behind children's behaviour (Conrad and Barker, 2010).

However, Burns (2013) suggests that a psychiatric diagnosis may be the only passport to the warmth, shelter attention and affection previously or never available from family members (2013: 230). Indeed, the young people interviewed in this study were living in small household units where family break-up was typical. They were living in areas where the environment was challenging and friends played a key supportive role. It is difficult to see how the risky behaviours exhibited by the young people in this study could be helped by the attachment of only a clinical label. The young people in this study were not dissimilar from their friends raising the question of whether what was being observed was just normal variation – boys and girls growing up in a relatively common set of deprived circumstances, or pathological variation. Whilst some parents welcomed a mental health diagnosis, it was unclear whether this actually changed their children's offending behaviour. It was not possible within the evaluation of the YJLD scheme to explore what might have happened to the same young people had they not been brought into contact with mental health services though a gradual descent into the criminal justice system is the most likely outcome.

Over-formalising, or pathologising the antisocial and criminal behaviours of childhood could take the focus and resources away from diagnosing and helping children suffering from serious disorders. It has long been argued that criminals are 'sick' (Silber, 1974), and that crime is a symptom of disease (Flew, 1954) and in many countries psychiatry has been used for social, political and moral issues rather than medical needs.

Interestingly, the launch of DSM-V was widely criticised for extending the reach of psychiatry into everyday life. Taylor (2013) reported that new developments in neuroscience could make it possible to consider religious extremists as people with mental illness rather than criminals. She stated that 'we will soon be able to treat religious fundamentalism and other forms of ideological beliefs potentially harmful to society as a form of mental illness'. Radicalizing ideologies may soon be viewed not as being of personal choice or free will but as a category of mental disorder (Monahan, 2012; Bhui et al., 2014). Extending the scope of mental illness in this way fails to address the underlying social, family and environmental circumstances which contribute to these beliefs and behaviours. McLaughlin (2014) suggests that 'therapeutic justice' can focus attention away from the structural and economic causes of society's problems, as well as undermining the idea that individuals hold personal responsibility for their actions.

The question remains - does the pathologising of behaviours using the language of mental illness enable young people to move on with their lives or does it trap them in an over medicalised world in which they do not acquire the skills to cope with their circumstances? This paper argues that the value of orienting young people toward the mental health system rather than the criminal justice system depends on the perspective adopted.

Treating people and their behaviours with medication and therapy versus incarcerating them represents two ends of a spectrum. Tackling the fundamental inequalities which exist in society, and which remain inextricably linked to the kind of future that young people can access, may help prevent the emergence of some of these behaviours but relies on investment of huge resources and political will. Further qualitative research should try to unearth the ways in which 'mental health' or 'offending' labels affect young people's own perceptions and lives.

CRIMSOC 5: 'Pathologising Youth Development and Risk'

References

American Psychiatric Association. (APA) (2013). *Diagnostic and statistical manual of mental disorders* (5th ed.). Arlington, VA: American Psychiatric Publishing.

Barker, K. (1998). A Ship upon a Stormy Sea: The Medicalization of Pregnancy. *Social Science and Medicine, 47,* 1067–76.

Becker, H. (1963). *Outsiders: Studies in the Sociology of Deviance.* New York: Free Press.

Ben-Zeev, D., Young, M.A., & Corrigan, P.W. (2010). DSM-V and the stigma of mental illness. *Journal of Mental Health,* *19*(4), 318–327. doi: 10.3109/09638237.2010.492484.

Bhui, K., Everitt, B., & Jones, E. (2014). Might Depression, Psychosocial Adversity, and Limited Social Assets Explain Vulnerability to and Resistance against Violent

Radicalisation? *PLoS ONE, 9*(9). doi: 10.1371/journal.pone.0105918.

British Psychological Society. (2011). *Response to the American Psychiatric Association: DSM-5 Development*, British Psychological Society: Leicester.

Burns, T. (2013). *Our necessary shadow: The nature and meaning of psychiatry*. London: Allen Lane (Penguin Books).

Charmaz, K. (2006). *Constructing Grounded Theory. A Practical Guide Through Qualitative Analysis*. London: Sage.

Chitsabesan, P., Kroll, L., Bailey, S., Kenning, C., MacDonald, W., & Theodosiou, L. (2006). Mental health needs of young offenders in custody and in the community. *The British Journal of Psychiatry, 188*(6), 534-540. doi:10.1192/bjp.bp.105.010116.

Coghill, D., & Seth, S. (2011). Do the diagnostic criteria for ADHD need to change? Comments on the preliminary proposals of the DSM-5 ADHD and Disruptive Behavior Disorders Committee. *European Child & Adolescent Psychiatry, 20*(2), 75-81. doi: 10.1007/s00787-010-0142-4.

Conrad, P. (2007). *The Medicalization of Society: On the Transformation of Human Conditions into Treatable Disorders.* Baltimore, MD: The Johns Hopkins University Press.

Conrad, P., & Barker, K. (2010). The Social Construction of Illness: Key Insights and Policy Implications. Journal of Health and Social Behaviour, 51(S), S67-S79.

Conrad, P., & Schneider, J.W. (1992). *Deviance and Medicalization: From Badness to Sickness.* Philadelphia, PA: Temple University Press.

Dowrick, C. (2009). *Beyond depression.* (2nd ed.). Oxford: Oxford University Press.

Dowrick, C., Frances, A. (2013). Medicalising unhappiness: new classification of depression risks more patients being put on drug treatment from which they will not benefit. *BMJ* (Clinical Research Ed.), 347f7140. doi:10.1136/bmj.f7140.

Eisenberg, L. (1977). Disease and Illness: Distinctions between Professional and Popular Ideas of Sickness. *Culture, Medicine and Psychiatry, 1*, 9–23.

Flew, A. (1954). The Justification of Punishment. *Philosophy, 29* (111), pp. 291-307. doi: http://dx.doi.org/10.1017/S0031819100067152.

Foucault, M. (1977). *Discipline and Punish: The Birth of the Prison*. New York: Vintage

Frances, A.J., & Widiger, T. (2012). Psychiatric Diagnosis: Lessons from the DSM-IV Past and Cautions for the DSM-5 Future. *Annual Review of Clinical Psychology, 8*(1), 109-130. Available from: Science Citation Index, Ipswich, MA. Accessed May 26, 2015.

Freidson, E. (1970). *Profession of Medicine: A Study of the Sociology of Applied Knowledge*. New York: Harper and Row.

Gibbons, R.D., Hur, K., Brown, C.H., Davis, J.M., & Mann, J.J. (2012). Benefits from antidepressants: synthesis of 6-week patient-level outcomes from double-blind placebo-controlled randomized trials of fluoxetine and venlafaxine. *Archives Of General Psychiatry, 69*(6), 572-579. doi:10.1001/archgenpsychiatry.2011.2044.

Giles, D.C. (2013). 'DSM-V is taking away our identity': The reaction of the online community to the proposed changes in the diagnosis of Asperger's disorder. *Health (United Kingdom), 18*(2), 179-195. doi:10.1177/1363459313488006.

Goldson, B. (2002). *Vulnerable Inside: Children in secure and penal settings*. London: The Children's Society.

Goldson, B. (2006). Penal Custody: Intolerance, Irrationality and Indifference. In B. Goldson and J. Muncie (eds.), *Youth Crime and Justice* (pp. 139-156). London: Sage.

Gusfield, J. R. (1967). Moral Passage: The Symbolic Process in the Public Designations of Deviance. *Social Problems, 15*, 175–88.

Haines, A., Lane, S., McGuire, J., E. Perkins, & Whittington, W. (2015). Offending Outcomes of a Mental Health Youth Diversion Pilot Scheme in England. *Criminal Behaviour and Mental Health*, 25: 126–140. Published online 9th June 2014. DOI: 10.1002/cbm.1916.

Haines, A., Goldson, B., Haycox, A., Houten, R., Lane, S., McGuire, J., Nathan, T., Perkins, E., Richards, E. and Whittington, R. (2012). *Evaluation of the Youth Justice Liaison and Diversion (YJLD) Pilot Scheme*. London, Department of Health.

Hagell, A. (2002). *The mental health of young offenders*. London: Mental Health Foundation.

Harrington, R., & Bailey, S. (2005). *Mental health needs and effectiveness of provision for young offenders in custody and in the community.* London: Youth Justice Board.

Harpin, V., & Young, S. (2012). The challenge of ADHD and youth offending. *Cutting Edge in Psychiatry Practice, 1,* 138-143. Retrievable from http://www.cepip.org/content/challenge-adhd-and-youth-offending.

Healthcare Commission. (2006). *Let's Talk About It — a review of healthcare in the community for young people who offend.* London: Healthcare Commission.

Healthcare Commission. (2009). *Actions speak louder: a second review of healthcare in the community for young people who offend.* London: Commission for Healthcare Audit and Inspection and HM Inspectorate of Probation.

Her Majesty's Chief Inspector of Prisons. (2006). *Annual Report of HM Chief Inspector of Prisons for England and Wales, 2004-2005.* London: The Stationery Office.

HM Government. (2009). *Healthy Children, Safer Communities*. London: Department of Health.

HM Government. (2011). *No health without mental health. A cross-government mental health outcomes strategy for people of all ages*. London: Department of Health.

Horwitz, A.V., & Wakefield, J.C. (2007). *The loss of sadness: how psychiatry transformed normal sorrow into depressive disorder*. Oxford: Oxford University Press.

Lader, D., Singleton, N., & Meltzer, H. (2000). *Psychiatric Morbidity among Young Offenders in England and Wales*. London: Office for National Statistics.

Lantz, P. M., Uchtenstein, R.L, &, Pollack, H.A. (2007). Health Policy Approaches to Population Health: The Limits of Medicalization. *Health Affairs, 26*, 1253–57.

Mental Health Foundation (2002). Mental health needs of young offenders. *Mental Health Foundation Updates, 3*, 18.

Merikangas, K.)., He, J.)., Bourdon, K.)., Brody, D.)., Fisher, P.)., & Koretz, D.). (2010). Prevalence and treatment of mental disorders among US children in the 2001-2004 NHANES. *Pediatrics, 125*(1), 75-81. doi:10.1542/peds.2008-2598.

Ministry of Justice. (2010). *Green Paper Evidence Report: Breaking the Cycle: Effective punishment, rehabilitation and sentencing of Offenders*. Retrieved from:

https://www.gov.uk/government/uploads/system/upload s/attachment_data/file/185947/green-paper-evidence-a.pdf.

Monahan, J. (2012). The individual risk assessment of terrorism. *Psychology, Public Policy, and Law, 18*(2), 167-205. doi:10.1037/a0025792.

Riessman, C. (1983). Women and Medicalization: A New Perspective. *Social Policy, 14*, 3-18.

Riska, E. (2003). Gendering the Medicalization Thesis. *Advances in Gender Research, 7*, 61–89.

Rutherford, M. (2010). *Blurring the Boundaries. The convergence of mental health and criminal justice policy, legislation, systems and practice.* London: Sainsbury Centre for Mental Health.

Satterfield, J., Swanson, J., Schell, A., & Lee, F. (1994). Prediction of antisocial behavior in attention-deficit hyperactivity disorder boys from aggression/defiance scores. *Journal Of The American Academy Of Child And Adolescent Psychiatry, 33*(2), 185-190. Available from: Scopus®, Ipswich, MA. Accessed May 26, 2015.

Silber, D. E. (1974). Controversy Concerning the Criminal Justice System and Its Implications for the Role of Mental Health Workers. *American Psychologist, 29*(4), 239-244. Available from: Scopus®, Ipswich, MA. Accessed May 26, 2015.

Spector, M., & Kitsuse, J. (1977). *Constructing Social Problems*. Menlo Park, CA: Cummings.

Szasz, T. (1960). The myth of mental illness. *Americal Psychologist, 15*, 113-116.

Solomon, E.,& Garside, R. (2008). *Ten years of Labour's youth justice reforms: an independent audit*. Centre for Crime and Justice Studies: King's College London.

Taylor, K. (2013). 'The Brain Supremacy: Notes From The Frontiers Of Neuroscience'. Talk delivered at the *Hay Literary Festival*, 29 May 2013.

The, L. (2009). Editorial: Health care for prisoners and young offenders. *The Lancet*, 373603. doi:10.1016/S0140-6736(09)60374-3.

Turner, E.H., Matthews, A.M., Linardatos, E., Tell, R.A., & Rosenthal, R. (2008). Selective publication of antidepressant trials and its influence on apparent efficacy. *New England Journal Of Medicine, 358*(3), 252-260. doi:10.1056/NEJMsa065779.

Whittington, R., Haines, A., & McGuire, J. (2015). Diversion in youth justice: A pilot study of effects on self-reported mental health problems. *The Journal of Forensic Psychiatry & Psychology*, 26(2). Published online 3rd December 2014. DOI:10.1080/14789949.2014.985694.

Note: The total of all vulnerabilities does not equal 100% as one individual could have been identified as having more than one vulnerability.

CRIMSOC 5: 'Pathologising Youth Development and Risk'